PROUD
to be a
BLACK MAN

Professor Spencer H. Boyer

Parfait Thierry Mbous

PROUD
to be a
BLACK MAN

Professor Spencer H. Boyer

514-201 DANIELS STREET
RALEIGH, NC 27605

For information, please visit our Web site at
www.pendiumpublishing.com

PENDIUM Publishing and its logo
are registered trademarks.

Proud to be A black man
by Parfait Thierry Mbous

ISBN: 978-1-944348-82-3

PUBLISHER'S NOTE

This book is printed on acid-free paper.

Dedication

To all African Americans, and especially to all Black men and Black women in the world, who have never given up while facing intimidation, frustration, and racism in order to become respectable people and inspirational role models for others to follow .

Contents

Preface

To have feelings of admiration for someone unexpected requires that you follow their actions, but more, it takes time for you to make a good assessment.

It is commonly said that good and evil are the primary reason human behaviors compel us to compare and judge others on various areas such as family and work, and equally between genders and different races. These indicators and attributes enable us to know each other well but they also allow us to discover each other's values.

Generally human judgments are either objective or subjective depending upon one's personal understanding of circumstances and events. Objectivity should be strongly favored as it serves as an example to describe the socio-cultural character that is part of the anthropological capital. This reality should be considered even though it can be difficult to maintain due to the undulating and diverse nature of mankind.

The year 2019 gave me the opportunity to observe a great African American law professor namely Professor Spencer Boyer. I developed an amicable relationship with this academician and scholar through him, I learned to listen and, have patience, and more, to appreciate the style and demeanor of a man who, despite the influence of the White race on American soil, remains proud of his own race. Since my arrival to U.S. in 2006, I have had the opportunity to know this professor. This twelve year friendly relationship has now developed a deep layer of trust. As an African from Cameroon, a Central African country that has experienced both slavery and European colonization, vestiges of those horrific events continue to impact the contemporary life of the country. Negative psychological consequences and its associated trauma of slavery and colonization resonate with many people in the world.

"Proud to be a Black Man" is simply a book that retraces the advocacy for self-love by one of the most accomplished intellectuals from American university. As professor of Howard University, his teaching career expands about five decades, and the myriad of students he has taught during his tenure will never forget his contributions to their knowledge of the law. These African American students, alumni of Howard University, unofficially called in certain circles the "Harvard Black University", have, over the years, left their marks in the judicial system in many courts across the country.

Professor Spencer Boyer whose actions do not leave me indifferent, gives me more pride as a Black man from Africa on American soil. He inspires me to love more the Black race while respecting the others.

Introduction

Despite having experienced slavery, lynching, racial discrimination in America, and self-doubt, the Black Man has never given up. To survive and live on American soil while engaging in professional activities and cohabitating with other races – including the dominant and influential White race, the Black man must continue to fight daily for his dignity through the love for his work, even during times of economic decline. The degrading mentality of people from other races does not prevent the Black man from recognizing his value and performing his job well. For every passionate person, especially a black person on American soil, work represents determination, engagement, creativity, freedom, and autonomy. This is accompanied by a joy that allows him to forget the constraints and channel his energy for the good of his employees and community.

I left Geneva, Switzerland in July 2006 for the United States of America, a country of excessive capitalism where time is money, people are proud to belong to their respective communities, and the impossible is still possible, I am proud to be a Black Man , in part due the motivation of a famous African American teacher, Mr. Spencer Boyer. On her fifth birthday, he marveled at my oldest daughter, Blessing Boyer Mbous, who carries his name as a middle name. His wife, Mrs. Prudence Boyer, who is White, purchased racially different dolls for Blessing as gifts. She wanted my daughter to pick the one she identifies with. To the delight of the couple, Blessing chose the black skinned doll, with which she shared similar physical traits. "To love and identify with a doll with black skin as a Black woman while respecting those of from other races is a sign of self-love" Mrs Boyer commented.

It is worth noting that what impressed me the most when I met Professor Boyer were the paintings and sculptures from different countries in Black Africa adorning the walls of different rooms in his home. More pointedly, the paintings that trace the history of the African American people from slavery to the emancipation.

It is important to know the positive impact that can be made by a Black Man who loves his race, culture, and history, and who is able to passionately impart his values. Professor Spencer H. Boyer has been working for almost half a century with passion.

Proud black man
Professor Spencer H. Boyer
and his works

I was very moved when I decided to write this book. It is true that I had already had the opportunity to publish a book titled "Never Give Up" about the life of this great teacher. Going to the source of the information is the surest way to get to the truth. That is the reason why it is my pleasure to share this description of the Emeritus Professor. According to the website of the University of Howard which better describes professor Boyer, I will simply dwell on his biography, and his works.

Spencer H. Boyer

Professor Emeritus

LL.M., 1966, Harvard Law School
LL.B., 1965, George Washington University Law School
B.S., 1960, Electrical Engineering, Howard University

Biography

Spencer H. Boyer is the senior-most faculty member at the Howard University School of Law in Washington, D.C., where he has taught for 50 years. He has served under 17 Howard University School of Law deans, as well as 7 Howard University presidents. He is one of the most senior law professors in the United States, and is the senior African American law professor in the United States. He received a B.S. in Electrical Engineering in 1960 from Howard University; a J.D. from George Washington University Law School in 1965; and an LL.M. from Harvard Law School in 1966. While at George Washington University, he was both a member of the law review and a member of the executive board of editors of the George Washington Law Review. At Harvard Law School, he was the co-founder and co-editor of the Harvard Civil Rights and Civil Liberties Law Review, today one of the most respected civil rights law journals in the country.

During his 50 years of teaching, Professor Boyer has consistently won student awards for excellence in teaching. During a period spanning six different decades, Professor Boyer has taught at the law school longer than anyone else in its 148-year history. He has taught in excess of 4000 law school graduates, including, in some instances, two generations of the same family. Undoubtedly, he has taught more black attorneys than any other law school professor in history. Included amongst students he has taught are county executives from Montgomery County, Prince Georges County, as well as a former mayor of the District of Columbia. He has also taught many prominent judges on the federal, state, county, and local benches, across the country.

Included among his former students are two university presidents. Other former students have gone on to have illustrious careers in sport, entertainment, and intellectual property law, as well as a myriad of other fields, in both private and public sectors.

In addition to his current course load, he has taught Civil Rights Law, Constitutional Law II, Entertainment Law, Business Organizations, Contracts, Federal Taxation, Municipal Law, State and Local Tax, Unfair Trade Practices and Patents, Trademarks and Copyrights. Professor Boyer is credited with establishing one of the first courses in Entertainment Law at a major law school, having taught this course since 1972. Administratively, Professor Boyer was the Associate Dean of Howard Law School for three years under Dean Wylie Branton and was the Director of the Howard Legal Intern Program for a number of years. He has been a visiting professor at the University of Florida, University of Iowa, and Antioch School of Law in Washington, D.C, as well as a Distinguished Lecturer on Taxation and Urban Economics at the University of Buffalo School of Law. He taught Entertainment Law and Contracts as an adjunct professor at the University of the District of Columbia David Clarke School of Law. He taught David Clarke for whom the law school is named when Clarke was a student at the Howard University School of Law.

Professor Boyer participated in the CLEO program (Council on Legal Education Opportunities), a program designed to attract minority students and prepare them for law school, at Temple University and the University of Toledo. In addition, Professor Boyer served as Director of six CLEO programs hosted at Howard University.

He is the recipient of the Georgetown Law Brothers Forum Award, given at the "Celebration of Black Men in Law," honoring the achievements of black men in the legal field. The awards were given to men who have been committed to excellence in three different legal areas: academic, government, and private practice. Among the many awards and honors he has received, the following is a partial listing:

Distinguished Howard University Faculty Author Award (2000, 2002, 2004)

Spencer H. Boyer Scholarship established by former students to be given to outstanding law students at the annual Black Entertainment and Sports Lawyer Association (BESLA) Conference.

<u>Spencer H. Boyer Annual Keynote Address</u> established by students to recognize an outstanding lawyer in the entertainment industry, with said attorney to give an address at the annual SELSA (Sports and Entertainment Law Student Association). (SELSA is one of the largest student sport and entertainment law school organizations in the country.) The keynote address in 2007 was titled "The First Annual Professor Spencer H. Boyer Keynote Address," in recognition of forty years of untiring effort and scholastic achievements by Professor Boyer in the field of entertainment law. Professor Boyer was also presented with an Award of Excellence plaque at the conference for his continued excellence in the field of sports and entertainment law.

He has received awards from SELSA and various organizations for the last ten years.

Among other awards he has received are:

- <u>Outstanding Alumni Award 2002</u> given by Howard Law School Alumni Association for the first time to a non-alumnus.
- <u>Outstanding Professor Award</u> (2005-2006)
- <u>Professor of the Year Award</u> (1998)
- <u>Student Bar Association (SBA) Award for Excellence in Teaching</u> (1976-77); (1977-78); (1978-79); (1982-84) (1983-84); (1988-89); (1989-90); (1991-92); (1992-93); (1993-94); (1998-99)
- <u>Outstanding Teacher of the Year Award</u> (1997-98)
- <u>Outstanding Teacher of the Year Award Class</u> of 1999
- <u>Outstanding Teacher of the Year Award-University Award</u> (1997-98)
- <u>Student Bar Association (SBA) Award for Lifetime Dedication</u> (1977-78)
- <u>Outstanding Teacher of the Year Award</u> (1975-1976)
- <u>Outstanding Professor Award</u> (1973-1974)
- <u>Paul L. Diggs Award for Outstanding Professor</u> (1972-1973)

- <u>Student Bar Association Award for Dedication to Howard University Law Students</u> (1970-71)

Professor Boyer also served as an instructor in the Howard University School of Law Summer Abroad Program in South Africa where he taught "Protection of International Intellectual Property" at the University of the Western Cape to both Howard law students and students from across the United States and South Africa. At the behest of the Jamaican Bar, he traveled to Jamaica and gave a presentation on "The Protection of Jamaican Intellectual Property" before members and guests of the island's esteemed bar, as part of the Howard Law School Jamaican Project.

The National Howard University School of Law Alumni Association voted to present him with their outstanding alumni award, which was later presented at their annual meeting in San Francisco, California. This is the first time that the award has been given to an individual who is not an alumnus of Howard Law. In October 2002 at the Annual Meeting of BESLA, three of his former students established a scholarship in his name in recognition of more than thirty years of teaching Entertainment Law.

To broaden his interdisciplinary approach to teaching, Professor Boyer attended extended summer institutes on Social Science Methods in Legal Education sponsored by the University of Denver and the Law and Economics Program sponsored by the University of Miami. He is a frequent participant at various conferences, including the World Peace Through Law Conference, held in Mexico City, where he presented a major paper. In addition, he is the author of many scholarly articles. Professor Boyer has been a frequent panelist at various BESLA conferences.

He has been the faculty advisor to many student organizations, including the Entertainment Law Students' Association, Student Bar Association (SBA), the Barrister (the law school newspaper), the Howard University Law School Scroll, and the Howard University Law Journal. He is a founding faculty advisor of the Bryant Inn of Phi Delta Phi Fraternity and has served extensively on university and law school committees. Presently, and for the last twenty five years Professor Boyer has served as chairman of the Admissions and Financial Aid Committee at Howard University School of Law.

In designing a recruitment poster for the law school, Professor Boyer coined the slogan now used in whole or in part throughout the university: "A tradition of leadership, the legacy continues." True to that tradition, in landmark litigation, Professor Boyer was the plaintiff in a home lending discrimination case against a leading Washington, D.C. area lending institution. As a consequence of that litigation, the defendant bank agreed to increase its loans to minority home owners, to require its employees to undergo classes and counseling in minority lending practices, and to allow an inspection of their minority lending compliance practices. Professor Boyer's case resulted in one of the highest monetary settlements in the nation to date by a lending institution in an action brought by an individual plaintiff.

In recent years, Professor Boyer's community service has included representation of a non-profit organization dedicated to the construction of a family-oriented theme park on Children's Island in the District of Columbia. As a consultant to Trans Urban East Inc., Professor Boyer helped design the concept of tenant management and ownership of public housing. A partial listing of public interest organizations represented by Professor Boyer includes: Change, Inc. (an antipoverty agency), City-Wide

National Capital Housing Authority Tenants Union and the NAACP-Southern Christian Leadership Conference (SCLC), Poor Peoples Campaign. In addition, Professor Boyer has served on various boards of directors, including WETA (Public Television); the Task Force for Secondary Education, Montgomery County; the Federal Bar Association of the District of Columbia; and the Boys and Girls Club of Takoma Park. Professor Boyer also served as a consultant to the Department of Agriculture on civil rights and secured a grant for the law school, culminating in a paper on the enforcement of civil rights in the Department of Agriculture. Professor Boyer is listed in Who's Who in Legal America, Who's Who in American Law and Who's Who Among African-Americans.

Professor Boyer has also represented clients in the sports/entertainment field. A partial listing of his clients include William Becton and Friends (gospel stars); Harolyn Blackwell, with the Metropolitan Opera, who starred in the Broadway production of "Candide"; various jazz artists, including Dick Morgan; rappers and R & B artists; graphic artist Poncho Brown; and sports professionals such as Ross Browner of the Cincinnati Bengals; and noted boxers, as well as Dave Jacobs, the trainer for Sugar Ray Leonard, and the parents of Len

Bias. Professor Boyer also was involved as counsel in the historic Watergate case, ultimately on the brief of *United States v. Nixon* before the United States Supreme Court.

Professor Boyer is married to an attorney, Prudence Bushnell. Two of his three sons are attorneys, with one working in the Obama administration on European affairs and national security matters and the other working as a private sector consultant. His third son is a writer. He has three daughters. One is a software test engineer with a major company in Virginia where she utilizes her two degrees in Electrical Engineering and Symbolic Systems; the other two are middle and upper school students at Sandy Springs Friends School and Edmund Burke School, respectively.

Professor Boyer's office is located in 404 Houston Hall and he can be reached at (202) 806-8019.

Professional Contributions:

Policy Management Systems - Vista, a private antipoverty agency. Designed and structured individual public housing tenant councils and city-wide tenants union (1968)

Organization for Social and Technical Innovation. Designed and structured Tenant Management and Tenant Ownership Corporation for Public Housing (1969)

Trans Urban East Inc. - Designed and structured Tenant Management and Tenant Ownership Corporation for Public Tenants (1970)

United States House of Representatives District Committee (1974)

District of Columbia Law Revision Commission (Proposed structure for Alternative Sentencing, 1977)

Office of the Peoples Counsel, Public Service Commission (Rate structure for Telephone Company, 1980)

Publications

Federal Injunctive Relief: A Counterpoise Against State Criminal Prosecution Designed to Deter the Exercise of Preferred Constitutional Rights, 13 Howard Law Journal 51 (1966)

Commercial Success as Evidence of Patentability, 37 Fordham 573; (1969). Reprinted in 2 Patent Law Review 1 (1970)

Copyright Symposium, 16 Howard Law Journal 439; (1971)

On the Brief for John D. Ehrlichman, United States of America v. Richard M. Nixon, President. In the Supreme Court of the United States (1974)

Taxes and Social Policies, 1 Consumer Strategy, January, 1975

Administration of the Tax System: The Tax Man Cometh, 3 Consumer Strategy, March 1975

Expanding Liberties, Book Review, 13 Howard Law Journal, 459 (1967)

Housing Development and Municipal Costs, Book Review, 18 Howard Law Journal (1974)

Standards for Compensatory Damages Under The Civil Rights Act of 1991, Principal Investigator for Grant from United States Department of Agriculture (1995)

Professional Contributions

public housing tenant councils and city-wide tenants union (1968)

Organization for Social and Technical Innovation. Designed and structured Tenant Management and Tenant Ownership Corporation for Public Housing (1969)

Trans Urban East Inc. - Designed and structured Tenant Management and Tenant Ownership Corporation for Public Tenants (1970)

United States House of Representatives District Committee (1974)

District of Columbia Law Revision Commission (Proposed structure for Alternative Sentencing, 1977)

Office of the Peoples Counsel, Public Service Commission
(Rate structure for Telephone Company, 1980)

32

Understand Who You Are

As a maintenance Engineer in a Washington DC hotel since 2008, I never imagined what a wall of Lobby or room painted in black would look like, or the emotions it would generate in an establishment where customers come to rest and rejuvenate their spirit. It is worth emphasizing that is an impressive décor, which plunges individuals into another universe like a giant cinema screen. Stella Polaris, a French artist who explores black and white drawings states that, "Painting a single wall in black is a great way to highlight, in a very dynamic way, everything in its vicinity (chimney, furniture, paintings, etc.)"

I admit that when Mr. Awet, the hotel director, decided on a whim to entrust me with this task of painting white wall black, I thought that it was surely due to his ancestry. He is African American of Eritrean descent with a dark skin tone. I had doubts about the appeal of black as a color on a wall, and of its beauty in the largest presidential suite of the hotel (Room 1110), and in the large hall where customers are welcomed and rest after a hard day of work. All I needed to do was paint the wall, regardless of the details, and follow the instructions provided by the head of my chief of department, an African American named Mr. Bobby Black. By carefully applying myself as an artist determined to produce art work, a magical universe was born. Above all, it attracted the curiosity of customers who enjoy spending more time in those spaces illuminated by a bright light for their family or friendly gathering, professional meetings or dates.

Black Wall painted by Parfait Thierry Mbous (Maintenance Mechanic Engineer since 2008) - Washington, DC, November 2017

These spaces painted in black created an amazing and unique interior that is both dark, soft, and conducive to the creation of an atmosphere of relaxation and rest. Daring to paint walls in black is a part of "Black Attitude." In fashion, the color black is considered the neutral tone per excellence. According to the interior designer Marie Degante, "a wall painted in black provides a spectacular effect in a room and even in small doses."

The love of the color black pervades Professor Spencer Boyer's environment. Apart from African art paintings retracing the slave trade, and the emancipation of African Americans in the United States, one of most amazing things that I ever seen was a black porcelain sink and toilet in oneof the bathrooms in his villa. These items caught my attention because I have always seen them in white or brown. One cannot ignore that worldwide, celebrities from the worlds of cinema, music, sports, and business men and women get themselves noticed by being driven in luxury black cars. This preference is also extended to Professor Boyer whose cars are black in color.

Being proud of being a Black Man will start by loving the color black through multiple objects while creating a positive psychological value that will stay forever. The most effective method is to teach the little ones to get acquainted with toys that have the physical characteristics of a Black man and Professor Spencer Boyer, as an African American man, does this quite often during Christmas and birthdays for my children. This encourages me to continue offering black toys to my children.

This positive perception and appreciation of the black skin is a personal work where each individual gives the best of themselves. The result can lead to a pleasant situation where the Black person is always enthusiastic and comfortable in their skin while developing very good relationships with people from other races. Using a few tips to create a pleasant climate in the family and workplace would encourage people to assert themselves and their talents. It should be noted that from my early age to an adult past forty years old, I had the opportunity to see a doll that looks like the Black Man when Mrs. Prudence Bushnell Boyer, a Caucasian, offered a pretty Christmas gift to my daughter consisting of a Black pearled doll, with beautiful clothes, which caught the attention of all members of my family.

Arts and Culture

Living in ignorance would be like living with an incurable disease that's why we have to constantly research and the discoveries we make allow us to rejuvenate our spirit through highlighting moments that have changed the world.

No race in the world alone possesses the beauty of intelligence even though some inventions made by some races, particularly the Black race, remain unknown to the public. However, thanks to the internet, which is used by multiple communication vectors such as computers, tablets, mobile phones, etc., our contemporary world should restore the truth about great inventions especially those from the Black World, from antiquity to the present. Egypt, an African country ruled by Black Men and Women in antiquity, was the first world power, the cradle of knowledge where Westerners (mainly

Europeans), came to learn from Egyptian scholars who were mostly men with black skin.

Being an African American and a member of the National Museum of African American History and Culture located in Washington DC, I was fortunate to be reborn as a witness of history through the installation of objects resulting from the great inventions made by African Americans. A recuperation of about 300 years of history can be now corrected and proper credit given to the Black Men and Women who contributed to the improvement of living conditions in the world. Finally, inventors throughout history can receive public recognition as their work is attributed to them.

Education has always been the key to success. Humankind should continue to motivate the Black Man to know his art and culture, without discrimination because every human race is sacred and rich in history and value. I confess that apart from the great inventions made by Blacks in Egypt, I had no knowledge of inventions made by African Americans until I arrived in the U.S. in 2006. This was due to ignorance and the lack of available information in main stream education curriculum, and culture. I wouldn't have expanded my knowledge of the

African American contributions the world civilization if I was not lucky enough to meet someone who would direct my attention to that part of human history.

Being in possession of good information and keeping it for my self would be a crime. I believe sharing it would be better for the world. I cannot thank Professor Spencer Boyer enough for introducing me for the first time to the great inventions made by African Americans. I recall one conversation after I bought my second cellphone. While dining with him, he asked "Parfait, do you know who invented the cellphone?" I responded, "I'm sure it's an American." He continued, "It's an African American, Mr. Henry Sampson on July 6, 1971." Emotional, I responded that I didn't know. Professor Boyer proceeded to teach me the history behind the cellphone from his knowledge while using his laptop to support his claims. As a university professor and having served as an Associate Dean of a Law School, Professor Spencer Boyer knows a lot about inventions produced by African Americans. He has shared that knowledge continuously throughout his career and he was sharing it with me. It was a source of pride for him but also for the African American community to share accomplishments that would paint the Black Man in America under a positive light. He continues to share his knowledge in places as far as South Africa where he taught at the university level for a few months.

It must be emphasized that those living in Third World Countries like in Africa (cradle of the Black Man on earth) do not have the chance to know deeply the value and contributions of the Black Man because most historical documents speak only of the European civilization, thus of the White man. This gap should be bridged and rectified through documents housed and displayed in libraries, and museums. Correct depictions of Black accomplishments in human history would encourage Black people to get better acquainted with their values in order to have an open mind. I admit that when I became a member of the African Museum in 2012 and especially when I witnessed the inauguration of the museum located in the heart of the Federal Triangle by the 44th American President and first African American President, Mr. Barack Obama, I was overcome with joy. Being born ignorant is not our fault but if we become ignorant, it is our fault. To share Dr. Martin Luther King's words, quote, "Nothing in allthe world is more dangerous than sincere ignorance and conscientious stupidity."

I would not know how to express my gratitude to Professor Spencer Boyer who always embodies the pride of a Black Man and the African American Museum which is the window to the accomplishments of the Black People.They allowed me to broaden my vision on the values of the Black Man in the United States.

Never give up

The U.S. 2016 presidential election was full of bitterness. The elected Republican candidate, Mr. Donald Trump, has used all denigrating methods to qualify the African American or the Black Man in general.Passing through reputable journalists to congressmen, congresswomen, and senators, just to cite a few, one of his most recent tweets stipulated to congresswomen who are Americans to "go back wherever they came from." More, it continued asking them to "help fix the totally broken and infested places from which they came." However, these harsh words did discourage the congresswomen under attack, but rather gave these American congresswomen the opportunity to educate people on not giving up when faced with humiliation tactics.

This non-respect towards non-Whites people, and more specifically the Blacks, continues to stem from the evolution of the society, even when a Black man has a respectable standing. I remember a little story of Professor Spencer H. Boyer when he wanted to buy a house in a subdivision only inhabited by Whites. He met all the conditions to acquire the property, and the shenanigans and the discriminatory treatment of the bank did not discourage Professor Boyer who used his law degree and legal knowledge to buy the house he still occupies today. In the same vein, my wife and I wanted to purchase a house in a neighborhood where most residents are Whites. Some of my relatives swore that it would be challenging for me to purchase a home in that neighborhood due to my origins. But thanks to the hard work of my African American – of Tunisian ancestry- real estate agent and my trust in him, we were able to secure a property in that environment. During that period, I was reminded not be discouraged because I'm African American.

Professor Boyer's second son named Spencer P. Boyer, shared one of his experiences on Facebook during the 50th anniversary of the assassination of Dr. Martin Luther King on August 4, 2018 as follows:

Spencer P. Boyer: So, dad, where were you 50 years ago when you heard the news that Martin Luther King Jr. was assassinated?

Spencer H. Boyer: I was a visiting professor at the University of Florida. I was the first African American law professor at a predominantly White Southern Law School. I had just come into my apartment after dinner with friends. The phone rang and the guy on the other line said, "We just shot Martin Luther King Jr. You are next. We know your wife and daughter are home alone when you are at work." I talked to my colleagues at Florida and Howard, who both agreed I needed to get my family the hell out of the there. So, I immediately flew back to Washington DC, where I would see the burning buildings from the plane, to rejoin Howard Law. Your mother and sister went to stay with your grandparents in Arkansas while I sorted things out."

This strong drive of being Black has given me more courage than before. I recall my first request to visit the FBI building on Pennsylvania Avenue on July 5, 2019. Truth be told, I was a little skeptical about being granted the authorization to tour the building as an African American from African origin. But the determination that Professor Boyer has instilled in me has always been constant in my mind. He always told me never to doubt in my qualities. I courageously made my request to the Senator. Let me emphasize that I have already visited the White House twelve times, but I saw FBI building as another stigmatization of Black people that I need to overcome. Curiously, during my visit, I was the only Black person in the group. Not that Blacks don't have access, but I felt the disparagement and the stigmatization towards Blacks could have discouraged some from requesting to tour this building, which is a source of pride for the American people. Similarly, when I am visiting the White House, I am always the only Black in my group. Sometimes, it is a curiosity to other visitors who are mostly Whites. They ask me "Where are you from?" I often wonder if it is to ask me how I got the tickets or just to inquire my origins.

A man's life is a reflection of his actions towards life's challenges. The desire to transcend the humiliations endured by the Black Man should not weaken him at all levels even when his chances of success are constrained. Since the September 11, 2001 terrorist attacks in the U.S., American immigration policy and hiring practices in the public, private, and informal sector require immigration officers and human resources administrators to conduct an in-depth background of applicants. The newcomer to the U.S. must demonstrate their ability to take care of themselves, and information provided on their application for entrance to the U.S. must be correct and verifiable.

Job applicants must answer background questions for job referrals, which can be unfair. Nepotism, favoritism, and racism, often eliminate brilliant people from consideration for good jobs, especially African Americans.

Although America has opted for this approach in order to feel they are knowledgeable about their working staff, the Black man must know how to manage any obstacle so that he can live as a proud member of society. Professor Spencer Boyer has demonstrated this in his career. His goals are to never be discouraged and to become an African American icon. Fifty years of teaching is in American universities is not just handed to anyone .This feat requires passion, determination, and courage.

The question that each Black Person must ask is how he or she can make their community, and even the world, proud of their actions, Knowing how to love being a Black Man is an act off the heart that should be fully embraced. As Dr. Martin Luther King Jr. states, "Faith is taking the first step even when you don't see the whole staircase."

Conclusion

Hard work is challenging but with endurance, goodwill, patience, and determination, one can experiences positive results despite obstacles along the way. Being an African American born in the USA or overseas, or simply being a Black Man living on this earth, and occupying a position of responsibility, such as Professor Spencer H. Boyer requires working with love and the ability to innovate.

Therefore, it is important for a Black Man to always be optimistic, look for the major problem to solve, be better than the others, and satisfy not only his community but those around the world. It is through that philosophy that Professor Spencer H. Boyer was able to convince me that he was a "Proud Black Man", because in my opinion, he wants today to be better than yesterday for the Black community.

Knowing one's culture is a good way for a human being to know what he's worth. It prevents individuals from having an inferiority complex towards others from different races because each culture has its own values that must be considered for the sake of all. It is in that context that Professor Spencer H. Boyer thrives.He has always considered African culture and art as means that allow him to always be a proud Black Man.

I was born and raised in Cameroon, a country situated in Central African, and becoming an African American in the United States was my dream that became a reality. I am black and proud as the famous musician James Brown used to sing in one of his hits "I am Black and proud." That pride became much more evident when I met Professor Spencer H. Boyer in November 2017 , in

the U.S. He has always considered me not just a friend ,
but like an adopted son.

That Father / Son relationship has allowed me to have
an open-mind on the value of the Black Man worldwide.
Prejudices, intimidations and frustrations endured by
the Black community since the period of slavery, and
the colonization of Africa, will never discourage me. The
inauguration of the Martin Luther King Jr. monument
and the African American History Museum in the heart
of Washington, D.C. have galvanized me tremendously
and removed doubtsI held.For many years, until my
arrival in the U.S.,I did not have the chance to know of
great inventions made by the Black Community .